DADDY, CAN I COME BACK HOME

By Preston Jongbloed

Please contact: Preston Jongbloed

Email: hello@legacypublishers.co.za
contact: +27 765068200

Cover Image: Kelly Barnes -
www.kellybarnesportraits.
Used with permission.

Publisher: Legacy Publishers

ISBN: 978-0-6397-4609-8

To my wife Tanya Jongbloed, thank you for walking this journey with me. You are my biggest critic and my biggest support. I can't wait to see the miracle unfold in our lives. Ahren you have been a joy to both your mom and I. We love you buggy and we excited to see what God is going to do through you

IN LOVING MEMORY

This book is dedicated to special people that is longer with us. Jerome Rapitse, Clive Cyster, Ivor Johannes, Morris De Klerk.

The day that I allowed my father, my father in law and my spiritual father to speak into my life, is the day that the Lord began to restore my setbacks. I dare not dishonour any one of them at the expense of honoring one only. They all unique and have been a blessing in my life.

To Charles Jongbloed, thank you for being a Father and grandfather that I can count on. You have steered my life away from the societal norms and that I will forever be grateful for. Daddy, thank you for being in my corner.

To Derek Matthews, Pops our relationship I treasure. You have played such a massive role in my life and for that I want to say thank you to you. You are my walking commentary. I want the world to know that you are so biblically gifted and sound. How you do it still blows my mind, but I always treasure our sit downs when we around the word.

To Apostle Theo Roman, my father in the faith. All has been said, but you played a massive a role in healing a young man from church hurt. Thank you for being a leader I can count on. I am looking forward to serving you and the West Reach Family for many years.

I am because of people like you all.

Love, Preston

6 And he will turn the hearts of fathers to their children and the hearts of children to their fathers, lest I come and strike the land with a decree of utter destruction. - Malachi 4:6

CONTENTS

ENDORSEMENTS

I have heard many sermons and read quite a few books about the story of the prodigal son in Luke 15. Not many have painted the context of the narrative. Preston has managed to "Rightly Divide the Truth", by sketching the background. Having this knowledge in mind makes it easier to appreciate this story that Jesus Christ articulated.

"Daddy can I come back home", is very relevant and a must read especially with the pandemic of fatherlessness. - Apostle Theo Roman

---

Daddy, can I come back home? A Must Read

Most Insightful

If you wondered why we men are so 'derailed' and 'dysfunctional' in the 'world' today, this book is a must read!

You will never see the world in the same way again. I haven't just learned more about 'Father heart of God' - this book has a Grace impartation.

Hope for the Church!!

Have you wandered through life wondering what was missing? Have you wandered through your Christian life thinking there has to be more than this? Have you ever thought what is wrong with the church? What is wrong with society in general? Have you ever wondered what was I created for, do I have a higher purpose on this planet?

This book will answer all of those questions and more. It will open up insights into our God as a Loving Father that many have never seen.

This book will shock many readers, amaze some, and leave any who read it feeling as though they have had an encounter with Father heart of God. The writer, Preston Jongbloed, has obviously connected with the Father heart of God and has been given a message that represents hope for a fatherless world without much hope. This is a must-read for anybody searching for meaning in their life or their walk with the Lord, as heavenly Father. - **Pastor Kenny Roman**

Daddy, can I come home?

The question in itself is one that when an absent father reads it, the reality is a few questions run through the corner of his mind.

1. Why did I leave?
2. Am I able to reunite with my child(ren)

Preston does an amazing job painting the perfect picture of hope and God's amazing love for us, that even in sin He sent His son to not only die but to save us.

Reading this book will cause you to come to yourself. It will also cause you to feel like whatever state you are in not only can a father return home, but so can a child. - **Corey Marchand**

_____

"In a world where Fartherlessness is marked as one of the greatest social ills this read/book/the author presents us with insightful keys that has the potential to turn hearts towards Repentance, Restoration and Reinstatement"

#may sons come to their senses and return....may fathers forgive, get running and open up their arms
- **Adrian Paris**

PREFACE

Most of my time of reflection happens during my commute from one client to another. On a recent trip to the West Coast in the Western Cape, South Africa, I began to earnestly reflect on the stability of the modern-day Christian family.

The world has experienced a few pandemics: HIV Aids, Hunger and most recently COVID-19. However, the biggest pandemic must be the issue of Fatherlessness.

I've been involved with youth development for over 15 years and have found that children from fatherless homes are more likely to be poor, become involved in drug and alcohol abuse, drop out of school, and suffer from health and emotional problems. Boys are more likely to become involved in crime, and girls are more likely to become pregnant as teens.

The plan of Satan is to wreak havoc in families; the first institution that God created. To destroy the family, and to destroy a nation.

The world is seeking for answers, and as Christians we have a proven solution; the Love of God.

> 5 "A father of the fatherless, a defender of widows, Is God in His holy habitation. 6 God sets the solitary in families; He brings out those who are bound into prosperity; But the rebellious dwell in a dry land". - Psalm 68:5-6

INTRODUCTION

So God created man in his own image, in the image of God he created him; male and female he created them. – Genesis 1:27

We have been taught that God created man in His image. How often have we found that our natural instinct is to view God through the eyes of our earthly father?

To those that had stable, present fathers, our memories would be that of security, strength and feelings of warm and happy moments. This won't harm us to then view God in the same manner. For others with abusive or absent fathers, the very word father can be a razor wire barrier in relating to father God.

This has led to many of us struggling to see Father God as a loving father.

If we want to overcome the societal challenges we are faced with, it will start with fathers.

Journey with me through these stories found in the Bible:

1. The story distinction between the northern and southern kingdoms of Israel.
2. David's choices had repercussions for Absalom.
3. The story of the prodigal son and his father.

The fathers' decisions build a case towards how we see each individual carve out different paths.

The question many sons and daughters have in their low place is, "Daddy, can I come back home". The position of our heart determines how many of these stories end.

Section One
A FLAWED FAMILY

Absalom was the third son of King David. He never expected to be king due to his illegitimate birth and having older brothers, but he became one of the greatest men in Israel. Absalom's mother was Maacah

> *3 "Now there was a long war between the house of Saul and the house of David. But David grew stronger and stronger, and the house of Saul grew weaker and weaker".*

> *Sons of David*

> *2 "Sons were born to David in Hebron: His firstborn was Amnon by Ahinoam the Jezreelitess; 3 his second, [a]Chileab, by Abigail the widow of Nabal the Carmelite; the third, Absalom the son of Maacah, the daughter of Talmai, king of Geshur; 4 the fourth, Adonijah the son of Haggith; the fifth, Shephatiah the son of Abital; 5 and the sixth, Ithream, by David's wife Eglah. These were born to David in Hebron". (2 Samuel 3:3-4 (NKJV)*

David loved his sons very much and they became mighty men. Due to their status as David's sons, they were given high positions in the government.

> *12 "But she answered him, "No, my brother, do not [a]force me, for no such thing should be done in Israel. Do not do this disgraceful thing! 13 And I, where could I take my shame? And as for you, you would be like one of the fools in Israel. Now therefore, please speak to the king; for he will not withhold me from you." 14 However, he would not heed her voice; and being stronger than she, he forced her and lay with her". - 2 Samuel 13: 12-14*

Absalom had a beautiful sister named Tamar, who was a virgin. Another of David's sons, Amnon, who was their half-brother fell in love with Tamar and raped her.

The law was clear about the penalty for such an evil act.

> *16 "If a man seduces a virgin who is not engaged to anyone and has sex with her, he must pay the customary bride price and marry her. 17 But if her father refuses to let him marry her, the man must still pay him an amount equal to the bride price of a virgin. – Exodus 22:16 (NLT)*

After raping her, he rejected her with disgrace. This effected Absalom in a great way as this was his sister. His anger was first towards his brother and then towards his father.

Chapter One

THE FATHER CAUSED THE RAGE

Failing to deal with Amnon's actions.
Absalom had a right to expect David both as father and as king to provide justice for Tamar and due punishment to Amnon.

> *21 When King David heard all this, he was furious. 22 And Absalom never said a word to Amnon, either good or ba d; he hated Amnon because he had disgraced his sister Tamar. – 2 Samuel 13:2*1

David was very angry but there is no mention of any action. In Absalom's mind, being furious was not enough. As father, David was supposed to protect Tamar, but he failed her as a father.

David had every right to be angry. Justice for Tamar was what Absalom was after. Amnon should have been punished and Tamar exonerated.

David failed to share in his son's rejoicing.

> *23 Two years later, when Absalom's sheepshearers were at Baal Hazor near the border of Ephraim, he invited all the king's sons to come there. 24 Absalom went to the king and said, "Your servant has had shearers come. Will the king and his attendants please join me?"25 "No, my son," the king replied. "All of us should not go; we would only be a burden to you." Although Absalom urged him,*

he still refused to go but gave him his blessing. 26 Then Absalom said, "If not, please let my brother Amnon come with us." 2 Samuel 13:23 - 26

David had a suspicion that Absalom had an ulterior motive, however, David didn't realize the extent of Absalom's hatred until he was briefed by Jonadab about what had transpired.

28 Absalom ordered his men, "Listen! When Amnon is in high spirits from drinking wine and I say to you, 'Strike Amnon down,' then kill him. Don't be afraid. Haven't I given you this order? Be strong and brave." 29 So Absalom's men did to Amnon what Absalom had ordered. Then all the king's sons got up, mounted their mules and fled. – 2 Samuel 13: 28 – 29

David failed to act when Absalom fled from killing Amnon.

David developed a habit of doing nothing. In the case of Absalom killing his brother, David had a choice; he could have shown love, he could have shown justice, he could have shown both, but he did nothing. Absalom fled and went to Geshur where he stayed for three years.

Chapter Two

ABSALOM'S RETURN

Years later Absalom was brought back home by his father. A woman by the name of Tekoa was used to manipulate David into bringing Absalom back home

14 Joab son of Zeruiah knew that the king's heart longed for Absalom. 2 So Joab sent someone to Tekoa and had a wise woman brought from there. He said to her, "Pretend you are in mourning. Dress in mourning clothes, and don't use any cosmetic lotions. Act like a woman who has spent many days grieving for the dead. 3 Then go to the king and speak these words to him." And Joab put the words in her mouth.4 When the woman from Tekoa went[a] to the king, she fell with her face to the ground to pay him honor, and she said, "Help me, Your Majesty!"5 The king asked her, "What is troubling you?"She said, "I am a widow; my husband is dead. 6 I your servant had two sons. They got into a fight with each other in the field, and no one was there to separate them. One struck the other and killed him. 7 Now the whole clan has risen up against your servant; they say, 'Hand over the one who struck his brother down, so that we may put him to death for the life of his brother whom he killed; then we will get rid of the heir as well.' They would put out the only burning coal I have left, leaving my husband neither name nor descendant on the face of the earth."8 The king said to the woman,

"Go home, and I will issue an order in your behalf."9 But the woman from Tekoa said to him, "Let my lord the king pardon me and my family, and let the king and his throne be without guilt."10 The king replied, "If anyone says anything to you, bring them to me, and they will not bother you again."11 She said, "Then let the king invoke the LORD his God to prevent the avenger of blood from adding to the destruction, so that my son will not be destroyed.""As surely as the LORD lives," he said, "not one hair of your son's head will fall to the ground."12 Then the woman said, "Let your servant speak a word to my lord the king.""Speak," he replied.13 The woman said, "Why then have you devised a thing like this against the people of God? When the king says this, does he not convict himself, for the king has not brought back his banished son? 14 Like water spilled on the ground, which cannot be recovered, so we must die. But that is not what God desires; rather, he devises ways so that a banished person does not remain banished from him.15 "And now I have come to say this to my lord the king because the people have made me afraid. Your servant thought, 'I will speak to the king; perhaps he will grant his servant's request. 16 Perhaps the king will agree to deliver his servant from the hand of the man who is trying to cut off both me and my son from God's inheritance.'17

"And now your servant says, 'May the word of my lord the king secure my inheritance, for my lord the king is like an angel of God in discerning good and evil. May the LORD your God be with you.'"18 Then the king said to the woman, "Don't keep from me the answer to what I am going to ask you.""Let my lord the king speak," the woman said.19 The king asked, "Isn't the hand of Joab with you in all this?"The woman answered, "As surely as you live, my lord the king, no one can turn to the right or to the left from anything my lord the king says. Yes, it was your servant Joab who instructed me to do this and who put all these words into the mouth of your servant. 20 Your servant Joab did this to change the present situation. My lord has wisdom like that of an angel of God—he knows everything that happens in the land."21 The king said to Joab, "Very well, I will do it. Go, bring back the young man Absalom." – 2 Samuel 14: 13 – 21

Absalom's return was contrary to that of the prodigal son:

- On returning to his father, he was not received.
- Neither was his father waiting for him.
- For 3 years Absalom was refused an audience with his father.
- Absalom on his return was neither restored nor forgiven.

- There was a limit to the mercy David gave him.

David caused his son great strife, and this eventually led to his rebellion and his death. As fathers our decisions impact our children and the greater society.

David failed to address the trauma that Amnon caused Tamar, and this led to Absalom rebelling and forming alliances to take David out.

> *15 After this, Absalom bought a chariot and horses, and he hired fifty bodyguards to run ahead of him. 2 He got up early every morning and went out to the gate of the city. When people brought a case to the king for judgment, Absalom would ask where in Israel they were from, and they would tell him their tribe. 3 Then Absalom would say, "You've really got a strong case here! It's too bad the king doesn't have anyone to hear it. 4 I wish I were the judge. Then everyone could bring their cases to me for judgment, and I would give them justice!" – 2 Samuel 15:1-4 (NLT)*

What might have been? If only foolish pride had not gotten in the way. "Like father, like son". David and Absalom sinned the same sin; both lacked the courage to say "I love you!" I am sorry.

I am convinced that the three greatest things for the healing of a relationship are Love, Acceptance, and Forgiveness. This story has got to be one of the saddest in all of scripture. A father and a son, both of whom loved each other, but died as enemies.

David's life was marred by ill decisions, that had repercussions on his immediate family and that of the leadership that he built. As a leader chosen by God, not only did David not deal with things effectively, but his decisions also caused him to betray his son.

Chapter Three

DAVID'S FAILURE AS A FATHER LAY IN HIS OWN SIN.

In taking Uriah's wife and then sending Uriah to his death David lost the respect of his family and his own moral authority. He brought the judgment of God onto his own family.

> *9 Why, then, have you despised the word of the LORD and done this horrible deed? For you have murdered Uriah the Hittite with the sword of the Ammonites and stolen his wife. 10 From this time on, your family will live by the sword because you have despised me by taking Uriah's wife to be your own. 11 "This is what the LORD says: Because of what you have done, I will cause your own household to rebel against you. I will give your wives to another man before your very eyes, and he will go to bed with them in public view. 12 You did it secretly, but I will make this happen to you openly in the sight of all Israel."*

David cried out for his son when it was already too late. He should have turned his heart to his son sooner.

> *33 [a]The king was overcome with emotion. He went up to the room over the gateway and burst into tears. And as he went, he cried, "O my son Absalom! My son, my son Absalom! If only I had died instead of you! O Absalom, my son, my son." – 2 Samuel 18:33 (NLT)*

Truth be told, could David have handled the rape of Tamar better? Could He have done better with the handling of Absalom in general?

The moment David failed to protect Tamar, was the moment David set Absalom on a destructive path.

Section Two

WORLD WIDE PANDEMIC

The problem that we are faced with is that our fathers or parents are not positioned to receive their children who are in wild living.

Fathers are caught up in moments of how the prodigals of the world hurt, embarrassed, disappointed, and dishonoured them.

Some fathers are out of alignment as they themselves are sons that have carried guilt because of wild living and have not returned themselves.

A home where a father is out of position, is a home that is at risk.

Chapter Four

THE DILEMMA

We are living in a time where the family is under severe attack. Have you noticed all the bad news and madness lately? One of the common denominators in most of the National News has to do with moral values and the state of the family. The family is at its worst at present.

In 2019 the Human Sciences Research Council (HSRC) and the South African Race Relations Institute (SARRI) found that:

- 60% of South African children have absent fathers and more than 40% of South African mothers are single parents.
- According to StatsSA, in 2018 many young children (46%) lived with only their biological mother, and 2% lived with their biological father only.
- They also reported in 2020 that 71% of children from female-headed households were multidimensionally poor compared to 53,6% from male-headed households.
- Furthermore, children who grow up in fatherless households are at greater risk of psychological issues.
- The research has shown that boys who grow up with absent fathers are more likely to display aggression and other hyper-masculine behaviours, which increases their risk for unhealthy relationships, crime, joining gangs, dropping out of school and addiction.

- Fatherless girls are more likely to engage in high-risk sexual behaviors, experience an unwanted pregnancy or find themselves in an abusive relationship.

I believe that fathers can break the cycle of negligence in their families and keep family history from repeating itself. It's not going to be easy, and it will require more than just a few fathers committed to their families to get the job done. It will require a movement so great that it changes the course of history in our great land. So many dads are "missing in action" that we are causing our children to be placed under a curse.

> 6 "And he will turn the hearts of fathers to their children and the hearts of children to their fathers, lest I come and strike the land with a decree of utter destruction". - Malachi 4: 6 (ESV)

What? Is this possible? Does He mean…strike all of the land? Yes! God is giving us fathers a serious warning here just like he tried to warn Aaron about his sons offering strange fire. I am not belittling moms and how they impact their children, but God has placed fathers in the position of having the greatest influence in their children's spiritual lives that will carry all the way into adulthood. He will hold us dads responsible. We can bring a curse upon our family by our negligence and our absence. Now, maybe God's warning that He will "strike the land with a decree of utter destruction" makes more sense.

"As the family goes, so goes the nation and so goes the whole world in which we live". — John Paul II

Chapter Five

DEAR FATHERS

A few years back whilst working in prison, I facilitated the program, "The world needs a father". Every week the session would become very intense and would stir up negative emotions within the young men who attended the program.

One session that is particularly engraved in my head was when we were talking about "How do you see your father?". I allowed the men to share and as they were going around the circle, I consistently heard things like, monster, abusive, abandonment, evil and so many words that made fathers look very weak and dangerous.

As we came to the last young man, he started with barely any words coming out of his mouth, because he was crying uncontrollably. He had a very real moment of realization of what these men were saying about their fathers.

"Preston, I am a father, is that what my girls are saying about me? I am stuck behind bars, leaving them vulnerable, I am repeating the very same cycle that my father created in my life".

Some of us have been blessed with tremendous models of what fatherhood was meant to be: a reflection of our relationship with our Father in heaven. But there are others who have been ignored, neglected, abused, or abandoned.

Our associate pastor, Morris De Klerk, used to say to me "Preston, our streets are bleeding because fathers are out of sync with their responsibility".

This could not be a truer statement. When the father is dislodged from the home and their children's lives, they cause disfunction.

> 5 "A father of the fatherless, a defender of widows, Is God in His holy habitation. 6 God sets the solitary in families; He brings out those who are bound into prosperity; But the rebellious dwell in a dry land". – Psalms 68: 5-6

This is God's desire for us that we take our position in our communities and homes.

One of the key things that I would do with inmates in prison was to hold one on one meetings calling it "Let's talk about your dad".

In almost all the cases the reason for these young men ending up in prison is because of "Father Issues"

> 4 "And you, fathers, do not provoke your children to wrath, but bring them up in the training and admonition of the Lord". – Ephesians 6:4

The cultural setting in which this Scripture was written was in Rome. Rome had a law called Patria Potestas.

Patria Potestas, (Latin: "power of a father") - in Roman family law, power that the male head of a family exercised over his children and his more remote descendants in the male line, whatever their age, as well as over those brought into the family by adoption. This power meant originally not only that he had control over the persons of his children, amounting even to a right to inflict capital punishment, but that he alone had any rights in private law. Thus, acquisitions of a child became the property of the father. The father might allow a child (as he might a slave) certain property to treat as his own, but in the eye of the law it continued to belong to the father. (n.3)

A displeased dad could disown his children, sell them into slavery, or even kill them with no consequences.

When a child was born, the newborn was placed between the father's feet. If the father picked up the baby, the child stayed in the home. If he turned and walked away, the child was either left to die or sold at auction.

The position of the father in a child's life is key to the outcome of that child's wellbeing. How many fathers have disowned their children, left them vulnerable, and caused them to be bound as slaves to poverty, or even killed their futures with no consequences.

Or are things better today?

This verse begins: "And you, fathers."

Apostle Paul outlined the biblical roles of husbands and wives in chapter 5. Chapters 6, he highlights the importance of children obeying and honouring their parents. And now he moves to fathers. The word "you" is assertive, as if he's calling out dads in order to get their attention. This can also be seen as a serious moment.

Apostle Paul addresses fathers here because he knows that we especially need to hear this. In essence we're challenged to see the word "fathers" as a verb, not just a noun. It's biologically easy to become a father, but biblically challenging to actually "father" our children. In this passage, we're given one important caution and a few commands that are as important.

The Caution
The first statement is negatively positioned,

 "Do not provoke your children to wrath". Another version says, "Do not exasperate your children." God starts with a negative command because He knows that fathers, who are fallen creatures, are prone to abuse their authority in the home.

The Greek word translated "provoke" means "to rouse to anger, to enrage, irritate or embitter." The present tense of the verb indicates that we are to stop doing something that is common and continuous. This warning is calling us dads to avoid anything that will eventually break the spirit of our children.

> 21 "Fathers, do not provoke your children, lest
> they become discouraged". - Colossians 3:21

Remember that our children are commanded by God to honor us. When we provoke them to wrath, we are causing them to break the Fifth Commandment. In such cases we are guilty before God for disobeying His principles.

> 4 "Fathers, do not provoke your children to
> anger, but bring them up in the discipline and
> instruction of the Lord". - Ephesians 6:4

The question beckons, how do we provoke our children to anger:

Overprotection.
Laban, an Old Testament dad, was an overprotective and domineering parent. He dealt dishonestly with Jacob in order to get him to marry Leah. Ironically, despite Laban's overprotective interfering, the daughters' assessment was that their father did not

really care for them. Listen to what they say about their dad.

> *15 "Are we not regarded by him as foreigners? For he has sold us, and he has indeed devoured our money". - Genesis 31:15*

Overindulgence.
The flip side of overprotection is overindulgence. Excessively indulgent parents are as likely to provoke them to wrath as much as those who stifle them. Studies show that children given too much freedom begin to feel insecure and unloved. Because our society has fostered increasingly permissive attitudes toward children, we are now reaping the harvest of a whole generation of angry young people who end up resenting their parents. Fathers, don't give your children everything they want. Related to this, guard against commitments that take your children away from gathering with God's people. You don't want them to grow up thinking that sports or other activities are more important than church.

Favoritism.
We anger children by showing favoritism. Isaac favored Esau over Jacob while Rebecca preferred Jacob. As a result, that family became fractured, and the two brothers became bitter rivals.

Unrealistic Goals.
Fathers, we can provoke our children to wrath by

constantly pushing perfection.

> *11 "For you know how, like a father with his children, 12 we exhorted each one of you and encouraged you and charged you to walk in a manner worthy of God, who calls you into his own kingdom and glory". - 1 Thessalonians 2:11-12*

Apostle Paul reveals a fatherly concern for the church: "We exhorted, and comforted, and charged every one of you, as a father does his own children."

While it's true that we're called to exhort and charge our children, we're also to encourage them.

Discouragement.
Fathers let's cut out criticism and sarcasm and look for ways to celebrate and affirm. Let's give our approval spontaneously so our children don't have to earn it or look for it elsewhere. Let's catch our children doing things right instead of always lashing out at them for everything they do wrong. Here's a simple rule of thumb: For every time you have to correct, equalize it with a word of encouragement.

Neglect.
Another way to exasperate your children is by neglecting them. When we fail to show affection or act indifferently toward our children, we can cause them to burn with anger. We can neglect our children

by never being home; or we can do so by being home yet absent from their lives.

Excessive Discipline.
Too much punishment is another sure way to provoke a child to anger. Dads, don't ride your children constantly. The father who throws his weight around – whether physically or verbally – can be devastating to a child's spirit.

Hypocrisy.
One way to provoke your child to anger is by not being a man of integrity. Children have a hypocrisy meter. They can tell when we're faking our faith.

Anger.
If you don't want angry offspring, then make sure you are not an angry man.

The caution is clear,

> *"Do not provoke your children to wrath." Now, let's look at four commands from the second half of Ephesians 6:4: "...but bring them up in the training and admonition of the Lord".*

The commands
The word "but" shows a contrast between what we should not do and what we are to do.
So, a few days ago my wife shared with me that

while she was doing the laundry my son Ahren was with her and they were speaking about heroes. He mentioned to her that "Daddy, is my hero". Our next-door neighbour heard that and commented to my wife how powerful that was. One of the things I love doing with Ahren is giving him tight hugs and counting till 10 before we let go.

I have no doubt that Ahren's comment relates to an incident we recently experienced. I took Ahren to the museum to see the dinosaurs and animal wildlife. On our way out of the museum, I was confronted by a group of men who was clearly looking for an argument. The conversation got really heated and I could sense Ahren was scared, and somehow between fending the guys off and holding him tight, one thing was clear; if it got physical, someone would land up in hospital and it wouldn't be me, as nothing would stop me from protecting my son.

The thought never crossed my mind to just "let him go". Here then are four ways to not let go. The commands outlined for us.

Command Number #1: Add value

The first thing fathers are called to do is to "bring them up". This is similar to the statement that is made about our wives.

> 28 "In the same way husbands should love their wives as their own bodies. He who

> loves his wife loves himself. 29 For no one
> ever hated his own flesh, but nourishes and
> cherishes it, just as Christ does the church,
> 30 because we are members of his body". -
> Ephesians 5:28-29 (NIV)

This is the same phrase that is used, referring to the husband's role of "nourishing and cherishing" his wife. We are to "bring them up." We are to bring our children up because they will not get there by themselves.

> 15 "The rod and reproof give wisdom, but
> a child left to himself brings shame to his
> mother". - Proverbs 29:15

All we have to do is look at the world around us to realize that our families are in ruins because, let's be honest, "Are you providing a nurturing atmosphere in your home in which your children can grow up to love and serve Christ?

Command Number #2: Educate.
This is a key command and important expectation: "in the training". This word also carries with it the idea of a rebuke or a warning.

> 24 "Those who spare the rod of discipline hate
> their children. Those who love their children
> care enough to discipline them". - Proverbs
> 13:24 (NLT)

If you refuse to discipline your children, it proves you don't love them; if you love your children, you will be prompted to discipline them. You may hesitate to discipline because you think it's unkind. However, when you don't discipline, you're not loving them.

Important Notice: Children need to be disciplined by their fathers.

> 11 "No discipline is enjoyable while it is happening—it's painful! But afterward there will be a peaceful harvest of right living for those who are trained in this way". - Hebrews 12:11 (NLT)

This verse speaks of God's loving discipline in our lives by showing how beneficial it really is.

It's important to understand the difference between discipline and punishment. The purpose of punishment is to inflict penalty and focuses on the past. The purpose of discipline is to promote growth by looking to the future. At the core of discipline is discipleship. There is joy in correction even though it hurts.

> "But consider the joy of those corrected by God! Do not despise the discipline of the Almighty when you sin". - Job 5:17

Command Number #3: Exhort.
We must enrich and educate and we're also to exhort. The word admonition is described in the Merriam-Webster Dictionary as: counsel or warning against fault or oversight.

We can admonish only after we're living it out in our own lives.

> 9 *"Only take heed to yourself, and diligently keep yourself, lest you forget the things your eyes have seen, and lest they depart from your heart all the days of your life. And teach them to your children and your grandchildren". - Deuteronomy 4:9 (NKJV)*

Let's make sure we're enriching, educating and exhorting. There's one more expectation.

Command Number #4: Evangelize.
All of this is to be "of the Lord." "Lord" is an extremely exalted title in the New Testament. To say that Jesus is Lord means that He is the rightful king of the universe, He is ruler over the entire world, He is commander of all the armies of heaven, He is triumphant over sin and death and pain and satan and hell, and He will one day establish His kingdom in righteousness.

- Raise them to know that the path of sin is a dead-end street and the only way to be saved and satisfied is through our Lord and Savior, Jesus Christ.

- Raise them to see everything in relation to the victory of God. Do whatever it takes to make all of life God-saturated for your children.
- Raise them to find their place in the triumphant cause of the Lord Jesus Christ.

Fathers are the point men in families. The coach of the team. The captain. Your barracks is the boot camp for training young soldiers for the greatest combat ever. Your residence is a launching pad for missiles of missionary zeal aimed at the unreached peoples of the world.

The goal is not merely to get our children to outwardly conform to a list of rules. The mandate is to develop children who seek to glorify God with their lives. It is not enough to teach them to do good things; our job is to teach our children to live on mission by gathering, growing, giving and going. Dads, you're the leader. Lead on! Your children are waiting for you to fight for them and to never let go!

Let's be honest about something.We have a problem, don't we? The reason why our sons, like the prodigal is left in limbo, is because our hearts are incorrectly positioned.

"And he will turn the hearts of the fathers to the children, and the hearts of the children to their fathers, Lest I come and strike the earth with a curse." - Malachi 4:6 (NKJV)

It's a heart issue. When our heart is fully focused on our children our hearts will be positioned to love unconditionally. This will lead to us doing a pretty decent job of fathering because fathers who are intentional make the greatest impact.

But there's something even more critical. In order to be a father who leads his children well, you must be a father who has placed his faith in Jesus Christ. If you want to be a good dad, you must be a growing disciple. There is no way to father in your own strength.

The state of our families is directly attributed to the fact that fathers have left their post.

During my time working in prison, there was an experiment done over Mother's day and Father's day.

The prison provided free cards to be distributed to inmates for Mother's day and almost all cards were taken. The same was done for Father's day, however, hardly any cards were used.

The calling of a father cannot be done apart from a

life in Christ.

The father in the story of the prodigal son is a type of Jesus Christ.

Chapter Six

THE FATHERS
WOUND

What is the father wound? Every person has a deep longing in their heart to hear from their father the same words Christ heard from His Father.

> *"This is my beloved Son (or daughter), in whom I am well-pleased". (Matt 3:17; 17:5).*

Every person has a deep longing to know we have pleased our father.

Absalom was puzzled about his identity – whether he was forgiven or merely tolerated. Whether he was now labelled as a slave or a dead son.When King David learned of the rebellion, he and his followers fled Jerusalem.

> *11 "David then said to Abishai and all his officials, "My son, my own flesh and blood, is trying to kill me. How much more, then, this Benjamite! Leave him alone; let him curse, for the LORD has told him to. 12 It may be that the LORD will look upon my misery and restore to me his covenant blessing instead of his curse today".13 "So David and his men continued along the road while Shimei was going along the hillside opposite him, cursing as he went and throwing stones at him and showering him with dirt. 14 The king and all the people with him arrived at their destination exhausted. And there he refreshed himself".*
> *- 2 Samuel 16 9 (NIV)*

Meanwhile, Absalom took advice from his counsellors on the best way to defeat his father. Before the battle, David ordered his troops not to harm Absalom. The two armies clashed at Ephraim, in a large oak forest. Twenty thousand men fell that day. The army of David prevailed.

As Absalom was riding his mule under a tree, his hair got entangled in the branches. The mule ran off, leaving Absalom hanging in the air, helpless.

A father wound left open will cause rage and could lead to our sons self-destructing - causing questions of unworthiness.

I have been confronted by young people on multiple occasions with the words, "I didn't ask to be here". We all enter this world helpless, dependent, and needing acceptance, to be treated as worthy, and to be blessed. The father wound, which refers to father absenteeism, whether emotionally or both emotionally and physically, and/or your father being very critical, negative, and even an abusive character, can impact individuals and their future relationships in so many ways. This behaviour is the absence of this love from a father.

The wound can be caused by: neglect, questioning who I am, am I unimportant, absence caused by divorce, separation, death, abuse effecting mental, physical, sexual and spiritual wellness, control through oppressive domination or withholding love, blessings and/or affirmation, deficiencies that lead to a profound lack of self-acceptance.

How does "the father wound" impact adult well-being and relationships? (N.4)

Low self-esteem & low confidence: Children are self-centred by nature. They often blame themselves for anything negative that happens in childhood and particularly if it is not clearly explained to them. Your inner critic (the internal voice) may be saying you are not worthy of good things, or you are not good enough (because your father left). Growing up you may have felt different as a child if all your friends had two parents and you grew up without a father.

Anxiety: There could be a combination of things and events that have contributed to you experiencing anxiety. Growing up with an (emotionally) absent father may have left you with a feeling of "I am not good enough" and perhaps you have hidden feelings such as a sense of loss, anger, shame, sadness and anxiety in trying to keep those deep emotions at bay.

Low mood / depression: Over time your anxiety can turn to low mood. On the other hand, you may have internalized your anger towards your father and him being absent and feel depressed as a result.

Anger & rage: Perhaps you have had the worst kind of experience with your father. Perhaps he used substances, was abusive, lied and was an unreliable man whose behavior deeply hurt you. You may feel like you are stuck in anger, and this can manifest in many ways. You may displace your anger that doesn't have an outlet somewhere else like experiencing road rage if it feels that it is not appropriate for you to express anger in other ways. You may also often feel anger and rage whenever there is a conflict in a relationship.

Too rigid boundaries: If your father has been unreliable perhaps by not showing up or even being absent from your life, you may have decided that you cannot allow people (romantic partners) to get close to you, so you choose to protect yourself. The pain of dealing with the aftermath of being let down by your father especially as a young child may feel worse than the loneliness rigid boundaries can cause. I recently wrote a post about "Is fear of being influenced by the other influence ruining your relationship?"

Too loose boundaries: You may feel that you have to be available to everyone else all the time. Perhaps deep down you feel that to be loved by others, you cannot hold your boundary and say "no" when something does not suit you.

Having relationships with emotionally unavailable

partners: Unless we are aware of it, we often seek the same dynamic in our romantic relationships as we experienced in our childhood. You may have an unconscious wish to repair the early father wound by having a relationship with a person that creates similar and familiar feelings within you as you experienced in your childhood. We often gravitate towards something that feels familiar because at least we know what we are dealing with. Being in a relationship with someone consistent and reliable can feel potentially emotionally threatening. I have also written a post about the impact of how early relationships impact adult relationships. If you often choose emotionally unavailable partners, you may experience a lot of relationship anxiety. The partner is unable to offer you the security you need, and you may end up engaging in various behaviors to get their attention, such as nagging, excessive messaging, oversharing or other behaviors that may feel unsettling for your partner.

Parenting – repeating the pattern of an (emotionally) absent parent: Parenting is hard and when you first become a parent you are flooded with feelings that may be linked to your own experiences of being parented or experiencing lack of parenting. You may distance yourself from your child and struggle to build an identity as a good enough parent.

Instead of going to the pain and receiving the healing we need, we tend to respond to life events by creating a misconception about who we really are.

Relationship to our birth father
When we hold a perception of our birth father as angry, violent,uncaring, indifferent, distant/with-drawn,absent/abandoning,alcoholic, condemning and/or critical, we tend to believe the following words about ourselves:

I am unworthy, stupid, incompetent, unloved or unlovable. As long as we accept these words as our truth, we will experience depressed, anxious and angry lives.

A father that abandons his child creates memories that places that child at risk of reaching his/her full potential as a life built on brokenness will perpetuate a cycle of brokenness. This is exactly where we are now as a human race.

Relationship to God the father
Often a person's image of God the Father is contaminated by the personal experience he or she has with the birth father. When misconceptions about God are present, things like: God is angry, judgmental, unhappy with me, fearsome, legalistic, quick to punish and slow to forgive are thoughts and feelings that we experience. Our lives will be shaped around this false narrative claiming:

• I am not good enough

- I am guilty/shameful

If we accept these words as truth, we will seek to perform and prove our worth through perfectionism and materialism or seek addictions to cover up the pain.

Addressing the father wound
There are four steps to addressing the father wound:

1. Understanding the heart of God.
2. Inviting Jesus into the wounds created by the birth father.
3. Accepting the truth about oneself as a child of God.
4. The heart of God.

Section Three

THE FATHER'S EXAMPLE

The two sons in the parable of the prodigal son represent the two houses of Israel – the house of Judah and the house of Ephraim. The house of Judah became known as the Jews and the house of Ephraim became known as Israel and the house of Joseph. These two "sons" of the father are clearly distinguished throughout the prophets as the two houses of Israel. An important lesson in Biblical interpretation is to recognize the distinction between the northern and southern kingdoms of Israel.

The departure of the "younger son" from the house of his father is described in 1 Kings 11.

11 Therefore the LORD said to Solomon, "Because you have done this, and have not kept My covenant and My statutes, which I have commanded you, I will surely tear the kingdom away from you and give it to your servant. 12 Nevertheless I will not do it in your days, for the sake of your father David; I will tear it out of the hand of your son. 13 However I will not tear away the whole kingdom; I will give one tribe to your son for the sake of My servant David, and for the sake of Jerusalem which I have chosen." - Deuteronomy 29-30.

Chapter Seven
THE PRODIGAL SON

Jesus in His writing used a parable to demonstrate that no matter how lost we are, no matter what made us lose direction, it's on His agenda to go and find the lost.

When we read this parable in Luke 15, we must do so in context:

The two central characters in this story are the sinners and tax collectors, and the Scribes and Pharisees. The sinners are called this because their sin was public to the community. The Scribes and Pharisees were the cultural elite and believed what your life looked like was far more important than the condition of your heart.

Jesus tells the parable of the lost sheep to show that the Kingdom of God is accessible to all, even those who were sinners or strayed from God's path. He uses the example of a shepherd who has 100 sheep, and one goes missing. The shepherd leaves the 99 others and searches high and low for the lost sheep.

In the parable of the Lost Coin a woman loses one of her ten silver coins. The woman represents God. The coins represent people. The lost coin symbolizes a lost soul that God will work endlessly to bring back to Him, rejoicing upon their return.

The parable of the Lost Son is the story of a son who was recklessly wasteful. Having convinced his father to give him his inheritance early, he squandered it all on wild living before coming home.

But, I don't think that's what this story is about. I don't think this is a story about a son. I think the story is about the father and his unconditional love for his son.

> *The story begins with: "There was a man who had two sons". – Luke 15:11*

The man is clearly the subject of this story, his sons are the object.

The story is about a father who is extravagant and recklessly wasteful with his love for his children.

If you study this story carefully, you'll discover that it can tell you more about God than you've ever dreamed. This story is one of the most important stories in the entire Bible, because it's the story of what the Heavenly Father is like.

If you want to know how God feels about you, if you want to know how much you are worth in God's eyes, if you've ever wondered if you have any significance in this vast universe, then this story is for you.

This story answers the question, "How does God feel about you?" Can I tell you about it?

The story is a story Jesus tells. It's the third story of a 3-part series as earlier mentioned. The story is a response to the murmuring the Pharisees were doing when they saw him hanging out with the good for nothings of Israel.

The Pharisees didn't like it that He, a fellow Rabbi, was tarnishing the reputation of all Rabbis by associating with the outcasts of society.

This murmuring and whispering does not sit well with Jesus. So, He turns to them and tells them about a shepherd who had a hundred sheep and lost one, and a woman who had ten coins and lost one, and a father who had two sons, and lost one.

For years I read this story thinking the son was the star of the story. My whole view of God was elevated when I finally saw that the father, not the son, was the star.

The story of the prodigal son is a story told in a five-part series.

- Part 1 is set on the family land. It's about the father dividing his property between his two sons. The abnormal request to claim his inheritance early.
- Part 2 covers what happens to the younger son in the far-away land, where he runs and entertains his reckless lifestyle.
- Part 3 describes the interaction between the

father and the younger son when the son returns home.

- Part 4 deals with the older brother syndrome.
- Part 5 is about how the older son returns? – Or does he? To understand that you must understand a whole bunch of rich first century Jewish culture.

Chapter Eight

JEREMIAH

Over the last 20 years I have been involved in Christian ministry through either preaching or Christian radio broadcasting. This enabled me to travel the length and breadth of South Africa, including overseas travels.

This allowed me to meet so many people along the way, with so many experiences and stories.

I have also been led to preach on various themes, but the one that has always stuck with me was the story of the prodigal son and that of Absalom the son of David.

During the last 10 years of itinerant preaching, the modern version of these stories has unfolded in so many encounters with people.

A few years back I encountered two exceptional brothers who were actively involved in ministry.

The younger of the two brothers, Jeremiah, grew in popularity within the music industry. He began to participate in the best local and international music events.

The more he grew in popularity, the more he became less involved in church.

Jeremiah was granted the opportunity to play at hotels in Dubai. This was a very hard opportunity to turn down, but as with all things in life, our decisions have consequences. It was during this time that Jeremiah was introduced to the fast life within the industry, which consisted of drinking, drugs, women, and no respect for money.

Jeremiah met a young Muslim lady by the name of Layla. Layla had the most beautiful features, and it was no surprise that he fell head over heels in love with her. He was living recklessly enjoying the night life and involved with a lady who was from a different cultural and religious background and still practicing.

Jeremiah was reared in the church and most of his musical experiences and training was based on the foundations of Christianity.

He became yoked to an unbeliever, a citizen of that country.

> *14 "And when he had spent everything, a severe famine arose in that country, and he began to be in need. 15 So he went and hired himself out to[a] one of the citizens of that country, who sent him into his fields to feed pigs". – Luke: 15: 15-15 (ESV)*

The trigger leads us to prematurely squandering our inheritance.

Chapter Nine

A WRONG
DECISION

> *11 And he said, "There was a man who had two sons. 12 And the younger of them said to his father, 'Father, give me the share of property that is coming to me.' And he divided his property between them". – Luke 15:11-12 (ESV)*

In this parable three characters are introduced at once: a man with two sons. This was a common enough occurrence. What was, however, very uncommon was the youngest's request to inherit his share of the estate prior to his father's death. What was even more surprising was the father's willingness to grant his request.

The father is portrayed as a very wealthy farmer, with servants and land. So, his sons would have enjoyed a privileged status within in the community. The youngest of the boys was not satisfied with his life and made a request to have all that he stood to inherit. He wanted it immediately.

We are living in a generation of wanting things now, immediately, instant gratification. At that point the young man needed to heed the red flags that he was on his way to a very low place, sooner or later.

In some ways he fits the modern stereotype of a younger son, "lazy, irresponsible, covetous, and greedy".

Inheritance laws in Israel were designed to favor the older son, giving him a double share, probably with the purpose of keeping a family's land holdings together and the family farm intact.

> 8 *"And you shall speak to the children of Israel, saying: 'If a man dies and has no son, then you shall cause his inheritance to pass to his daughter. 9 If he has no daughter, then you shall give his inheritance to his brothers. 10 If he has no brothers, then you shall give his inheritance to his father's brothers. 11 And if his father has no brothers, then you shall give his inheritance to the relative closest to him in his family, and he shall possess it.' "And it shall be to the children of Israel a statute of judgment, just as the LORD commanded Moses". - Numbers 27:8-11(NKJV)*

> 7 *"So the inheritance of the children of Israel shall not change hands from tribe to tribe, for every one of the children of Israel shall keep the inheritance of the tribe of his fathers. 8 And every daughter who possesses an inheritance in any tribe of the children of Israel shall be the wife of one of the family of her father's tribe, so that the children of Israel each may possess the inheritance of his fathers. 9 Thus no inheritance shall change hands from one*

tribe to another, but every tribe of the children of Israel shall keep its own inheritance". Numbers - 36:7-9 (NKJV)

17 "but he shall acknowledge the firstborn, the son of the unloved, by giving him a double portion of all that he has, for he is the first fruits of his strength. The right of the firstborn is his". - Deuteronomy 21:17 (ESV)

If there were four sons, the older son would receive two shares, with each of the other three sons receiving one share each. Typically, the older son would be the executor and assume the role as family head after his father's death. Sometimes an older son would decide not to split up the family holdings between the brothers.

On one occasion when a crowd was listening to such teaching from Jesus, there was one person who showed no understanding of what Jesus was saying. Contrary to Jesus' teaching, personal safety and security were his main concern. He wanted Jesus to force his brother to give him a bigger share of an inheritance they had received. Jesus was not a rabbi who settled disputes about the law; he was a teacher from God, and he was concerned about people's greed (Luke 12:13-15).

He therefore told the story of a rich but foolish farmer who thought only of his prosperity, security, and comfort. Suddenly the farmer died. Not only was his wealth of no further use, but it had prevented him from obtaining true heavenly riches. - Luke 12:16-21 (Bridgeway Bible Commentary)

Chapter Ten

THE PREMATURE INHERITANCE, PART 1

The younger son asks the father to divide his property between his sons so the younger can have his inheritance now. And he does.

At first glance, you may think that this is just a really cool dad, or a dad without many boundaries who was just putty in his children's hands. You may be right on both counts, but you'd miss the point of what really happened in this instance, because what Jesus was describing here would be scandalous to every person who heard it.No one in the Middle East would make such a request to their father. Because to ask for their inheritance early would be tantamount to expressing a death wish for their father.

In essence, the son humiliates his father but acting as though His father is dead.

Author Ken Bailey, who lived in that region of the world for quite some time wrote this, "For over fifteen years I have been asking people of all walks of life from Morocco to India and from Turkey to the Sudan about the implications of a son's request for his inheritance while the father is still living. The answer has almost always been emphatically the same."

…the conversation runs as follows:

"Has anyone ever made such a request in your community?"

"Never!"

"Could anyone ever make such a request?"

"Impossible!"

"If anyone did, what would happen?"

"His father would beat him, of course!" "Why?"

"This request means – he wants his father to die!"

One Middle Eastern writer, Ibrahim Sa'id writes, "The shepherd in his search for the sheep, and the woman in her search for the coin do not do anything out of the ordinary beyond what anyone in their place would do. But the actions the father takes in the third story are unique, marvelous, divine actions which have not been done by any father in the past."

"Divide your inheritance, so that I can have my share of the estate," is the request. And to everyone's amazement, the father does!

The next part of the story goes as follows,

> *"Not long after that, the younger son got together all that he had, set off for a distant country and there squandered his wealth on wild living". – Luke 15:13*

Most Westerners think he left quickly because he was a party animal, plain and simple, and that being in the same town with his conservative old man cramped his style.

But that's not his motivation for leaving at all. Notice that he didn't leave immediately. He left "not long after that."

Why? Because he had to liquidate his inheritance. He had to find a buyer for his portion of the family farm, his portion of the family jewels, his portion of the family livestock. And the only people he could sell to were other people in the village.

So, as Jesus is telling this story, his listeners were imagining this brash young man, going from door to door, trying to convince people who knew his father to buy a piece of the family property. All those folks knew that this boy had insulted his father, shamed him, wished him dead, and now he was doing the unthinkable – selling off property and possessions that had been in the family for generations.

At every turn, he's greeted with amazement, horror, and rejection. The family's estate is a significant part of a Middle Easterner's personal identity.

As the scorn mounts, he feels more and more pressure to leave the town.

So, he leaves as soon as he has sold the last of his inheritance. By now, the community is openly antagonistic towards him. There's been talk about shunning him, or publicly shaming him – taking some action to put this young, insolent upstart in his place.

As soon as all the negotiations are done and the transactions completed, the son leaves town and heads for the far-away country.

Chapter Eleven

WILD LIVING, PART 2

In the far-away country, this wayward son gradually descends into his own personal hell. (n.1)

One Saturday afternoon I found myself at a Spar store doing some shopping, when I ran into Jeremiah's parents. I had been to their church on many occasions. So, through my ministry engagements we formed a relationship, and I was happy to see them and in the same vein asked them how Jeremiah was.

I didn't expect their answer. They were devastated by his decision to move to Dubai as they felt that it was a decision that would cause severe pain and regret.

> 12 "Honour your father and your mother, that your days may be long in the land that the LORD your God is giving you". – Exodus 20:12

No matter the societal status of our parents, whether they are wealthy or barely making it, the principle of honouring our parents takes on various forms and a violation of this principle almost certainly will bring calamity.

Jeremiah's parents' disappointment was not so much that he moved to Dubai, instead it was that they found out that he got married to Layla and turned to another faith.

Growing up in church and raising their son in the Christian faith was important to them. They could not understand how he could turn his back on his faith.

When we disconnect from God, we leave ourselves vulnerable to wild living.

> 13 "Not long after that, the younger son got together all he had, set off for a distant country and there squandered his wealth in wild living".

He wasted his inheritance on wild living. And the citizens of this far-away country knew that.

They, too, were unimpressed with this frivolous young man who was now out of money.

The polite way a Middle Easterner gets rid of unwanted "hangers-on" isn't to come right out and tell them to go home, it's to assign them a task they'll refuse.

So, when the son asked for a job, one of the citizens offered him the position of a pig-herder.

This is another humiliating thing for the father and the family as it's a job no self-respecting Jewish boy could accept. Pigs were unclean animals according to the Law of Moses. Pigs had to be fed seven days a week, which meant he couldn't keep the Sabbath.

The night life swallowed Jeremiah to the point where his life was spiralling into a black hole, a place where substance abuse and sex was a common occurrence.

As time passed his marriage hit rock bottom, only this time Jeremiah and Layla already had a child.

The pressure of being a father of a child meant that the dynamics shifted. He now needed to provide, but during the time of wild living, Jeremiah built the reputation of being unreliable, and that meant that bookings for work was slow, and that meant money was drying up.

One morning after being drunk out of his mind he found a note from Layla.

"Dear J, I can't do this anymore, I've decided to go back to my parents and am taking your son with me. Please do not contact me".

This was reminiscent of the prodigal son. Sometimes God allows us to hit rock bottom.

The young son found himself in that place of depression.

It was in this hole of self-pity that he began to think honestly about himself. He knew there was no life for him in that foreign land, yet he couldn't go home to

Chapter Twelve

COMING TO YOUR SENSES, PART 3

All of us have at some point in our lives reached a low place. That could be because of our own choices, circumstances created by others or just what life threw at us.

> 17 "When he came to his senses, he said, 'How many of my father's hired servants have food to spare, and here I am starving to death! 18 I will set out and go back to my father and say to him: Father, I have sinned against heaven and against you. 19 I am no longer worthy to be called your son; make me like one of your hired servants". – Luke 15: 17-19 (NIV)

The low place becomes a real place to take a hard look. The prodigal son started asking the hard questions. The loneliness started a conversation of:

- Who am I?
- Why am I Here?
- What brought me here?
- What's Next?

It's amazing how complex issues can suddenly become crystal clear when we in a low place. A low place gives birth to "Coming to our senses". That doesn't mean that we are shielded from the consequences of our choices, instead we now start the process of restoration. The son compares his own condition with that of his father's hired servants.

He is starving and they have food to spare. And he is probably aware that the famine doesn't extend to his home area. He begins to compose a confession to say to his father.

It is his father and his father's way of life that he is rebelling against. He blatantly ignored and snubbed his legal and moral obligations to his father. He asked for his inheritance, so he doesn't have to grovel to anyone. He went away rich and affluent, but had to return home with his tail between his legs. The very person he was so conflicted with he must now apologize to. There is no other way. How difficult this must be! How humbling!

His apology includes four essential points:

1. The sin he committed against God. He confesses his sin against God for his moral failures and sinful lifestyle.
2. He confesses sin against his father for squandering property that legally and morally should have been conserved to support his father.
3. He renounces any legal claim to sonship. Though he is a son by birth, his father would need to use his older brother's resources to support him, since his father already divided the property. He recognizes that he has no legal claim to the rights of sonship. His decision disqualified him from future inheritance.
4. He asks to be hired as a servant at the estate.

While his father no longer legally owns the estate, he is still running it, and will do so as long as he is physically able.

The prodigal son worked out what he would say and how he should say it. When our decision is wrong, we have to be humble to know that rehearsing exactly what we need to say is important. So many apologies are not apologies at all; they are half-measures designed to admit some culpability but keep one's dignity and pride intact. To his credit, the prodigal son works out a full apology.

Now he begins to think creatively. He realizes that he can't go back home and ask to live in the family house as a son. But maybe he could go home and ask for a job as a hired servant. That way, if he works hard and saves as much as he can, he may someday be able to earn enough to be of some use to his father.

He comes up with a plan: he'll go home, admit he was a fool, and instead of asking to be reinstated as a son, he'll ask to be hired as a servant!

How many of us can relate to the narrative that starts in our head. When we are in a low place, we look for a way to just survive.

The plan has merit, except for one thing: even if his father accepts him on these terms, he'll have to face the wrath of the community.

Anyone who has left their family home knows that it is always difficult to return home unless you have succeeded. This guy has not only not succeeded, but he's also a miserable failure.

But his real problem is, how did the community feel about him when he left? They hated him. He disgraced them all by wishing that his father was dead and then by disposing of the family's property. Added to that, he lost all his money to despised gentiles. He had no solution for what he was going to do about the villagers when he returned home. He would simply have to endure the mocking and shaming they would give him as he walked through the town on the way to his father's house.

Like the son, Jeremiah now finds himself homeless, jobless, and abandoned by his wife and this new life that he ran to.

At once, he turned his thoughts to Cape Town, South Africa, the place of his birth, a place called Home.

He questions everything about home; what his parents would say, what the people would say, how would he ever get the people that he turned his back on to trust him.

Chapter Thirteen

THE FATHERS HEART, PART 4

"But while he was still a long way off, his father saw him and was filled with compassion for him; he ran to his son, threw his arms around him, and kissed him". – Luke 15: 20b (NIV)

This is where the father comes into the story in full force. The father, because of his experience, knows two things. Firstly, he knows that the son, because of his maturity level and the character with which he left home, is bound to fail. He knows that, if the son ever does come home, it will probably not be as a successful businessman, or in the case of Jeremiah a successful musician, but most likely as a beggar.

The second thing the father knows is that the community will not treat him well. Human nature will always remind people of their shortcomings.

Since his departure, all the community would have told him openly and repeatedly was that he should not have granted the inheritance in the first place, and that this son is selfish and deserves nothing short of death.

He knows that, if the son ever does return, that the first person who sees him would quickly pass the word that this outcast has come home and that a crowd would gather and likely begin to mock him and spit on him, if not hurt him outright. He knows that the son, in order to get home, will have to endure the scoffing of the crowd with every step he takes through the community.

The father is fully aware of the consequences the son is faced with. However, what he does to counteract all this is nothing short of amazing.

The father does five things that would all be considered outrageous in Middle Eastern society. They're all designed to protect and restore this son that he loves so much. This son who turned away from him and rejected him and wished him dead.

The first Action
The first thing the father does is, he runs. When word comes to him that his son has been seen on the outskirts of the community, the father runs to him.

Why is this so significant? Instead of letting his son run the through the fire, the father runs through the fire for him.

It's an outrageous thing he does, bordering on humiliating himself, because a nobleman with flowing robes never runs anywhere. He lifts his robe, exposing his ankles, and runs down the road, through the community, in front of all the community members. He humiliates himself.

One ancient Jewish writer writes this about running. He says,

"A man's manner of walking tells you what he is."
– Ben Sirach

A modern scholar writes this:

"It is so very undignified in Eastern eyes for an elderly man to run." – Leslie Weatherhead

Aristotle, the famous Greek philosopher said, "Great men never run in public."

Even though running is seen as degrading, this father runs to his son.

> *"But while he was still a long way off, his father saw him and was filled with compassion for him..." - Luke 15:20*

He was filled with compassion for him. That's how the Father feels about his children. He has compassion on us.

The father deliberately runs through the community. He knows that he's creating a spectacle. He knows what he's doing will attract a crowd. He knows they will talk about his humiliation in the village for the rest of his life.

Imagine this for just a minute from the son's perspective.

He knows his father lives in the middle of town and that the town hates him. He knows there is no way he can get to the father without enduring being mocked.

However, he is clear, he has to get to the father in order to become his servant. So, he sets his jaw, and he walks the last few miles towards the town. And sure enough, at first sighting on the outskirts of the community, word starts spreading. People were going to gather. He was about to endure the worst moments of his life.

That encounter with Jeremiah's family set in motion an opportunity for me to reach out to him. I remember when we spoke telephonically for the first time, he responded with:

"I'm in a dark space, I am filled with regret. My fear is, I seem like a joke. I am a Christian - to Muslim - back to Christian....what worth is there in what people see me as".

I remember his words, how deeply it moved me, and I responded with, "God will work it out, you have a call on your life that has not changed".

As the prodigal son comes to the edge of the community, he expects to see rocks and jeers and angry faces. Instead, what he sees coming towards him are the ankles of his father. To his utter amazement, rather than experiencing the ruthless hostility he deserves for what he's done, he finds a visible demonstration of the love of his father.

Second Action
The father threw his arms around him; this was a very powerful act. The prodigals of this world are so used to be frowned upon and judged, that the fatherly position breaks the mould and not only demonstrates love but affirms that no matter what your wild living looks like, I am glad you home.

The Third Action

> *The third thing the father does is, he kisses his son. "He ran to his son, threw his arms around him and kissed him". – Luke 15:20*

Can you picture it? They're embracing, eye to eye, shoulder to shoulder.

In his mind, the son had pictured himself coming home and humiliating himself firstly, by kissing his father's hand, then he'd kiss his father's feet. But the father wouldn't let him. He puts his arms around him and kissed him on both cheeks.

The son can't bend, he can't prevent this. All he can do is accept this love.

Look at the picture now. You have wronged God, and you know it. You know you're going to need to beg for forgiveness and admit wrong and make all sorts of promises and really mean it.

So, you approach Him. And you've got your whole speech planned. Only He doesn't even let you begin. The minute you approach Him, He embraces you. It's a powerful picture, isn't it?

> *Now, let's back up and see for a minute what the son had planned to do when he first saw his father. The son had this entire speech planned in his mind. He says, "I will set out and go back to my father and say to him: Father, I have sinned against heaven and against you. I am no longer worthy to be called your son; make me like one of our hired men". – Luke 15:19*

See his plan? Repent, admit his guilt, and ask to become a servant in his father's household.

Only the father has a different plan. This is what really happens,

> *21 "The son said to him, 'Father, I have sinned against heaven and against you. I am no longer worthy to be called your son'. – Luke 15:21*

What's missing from the speech? His request to become a servant.

Why is it missing?

Because he's overwhelmed by the father's love. His plan was to earn his way back into his father's favor. He never intended to ask his father to accept him back just as he was. How could he do that?

But when the father runs and kisses him, how could he not accept the father's love for a son?

The Fourth Action
The father calls for a robe to be put on his son.

> 22 "But the father said to his servants, 'Quick! Bring the best robe and put it on him". – Luke 15:22

Imagine the picture: Bring my reckless, wild living and drug user son the best robe.

The question that comes to my mind is: who owned the best robe in the family? The father.

David's response: He never asked for the robe, the robe is meant for honored guests.

Absalom was merely tolerated, even David's kiss was mere show and formality. Restoration requires authenticity.

The father of the prodigal son finds himself standing on the edge of the community, and the father wants the whole community to know that he has accepted his son. So, he sends his servants to get his own best robe so the son can wear it as he walks home through the entire community.

The Fifth Action

> *The father called for a ring. "Put a ring on his finger and sandals on his feet". – Luke 15:22b (NIV)*

Absalom does not receive the ring; however, the prodigal son receives the ring to signify the restoration back to the family.

The ring is probably a signet ring. It's the ring the father would use to sign all documents, which means the son is a trusted, empowered member of the family.

Absalom did not get the sandals. The sandals were only meant for sons. The servants did not wear sandals. The sandals are a sign he is a free man, not a servant. Servants didn't wear shoes. They walked barefoot.

The Last Action

> 23 "Bring the fattened calf and kill it. Let's have a feast and celebrate. 24 For this son of mine was dead and is alive again; he was lost and is found.' So they began to celebrate". – Luke 15:23- 24

The father was very specific with his request, He didn't ask for the fatted goat or sheep or chicken.

Instead, he asked for the fatted calf. Why a calf?

In biblical times, people would often keep at least one piece of livestock that was fed a special diet to fatten it up, thus making it more flavorsome when prepared as a meal. Slaughtering this livestock was to be done on rare and special occasions. Thus, when the prodigal son returns, the father "kills the fatted calf" to show that the celebration is out of the ordinary, because a calf had enough meat on it to feed the whole community.

The father's intensions are clear.
He's inviting the whole community to share his joy. He doesn't want the son only to be reconciled to him, he wants him to be reconciled to the whole community. He wants everyone to have a relationship with his son.

This is a story that no one could have anticipated.

For Palestinian listeners, initially the father would naturally be a symbol of God. Then, as the story progresses, the father comes down out of the house and, in a dramatic act, demonstrates unexpected love publicly in humiliation.

It is a rag to unbelievable riches story. Only the riches aren't about money, they're about measuring your worth in God's eyes.

Do you see what Jesus is doing with this story? He is communicating to every person who ever wanted to take a step towards God, how significant we are to Him. How God feels about us. He doesn't just wait for us; He runs to us. He doesn't let us bear the shame of living our lives as if we wished He bears it for us. He kisses us. He puts His robe on us, His ring on our finger, His sandals on our feet, He kills the fatted calf to celebrate us and invites everyone else to celebrate us with Him.

Since my meeting with Jeremiah's parents, I felt the need to reach out to him and just support him in a small way. Recently I received a distress call from Jeremiah.

"Preston, I want to come home, will you be there when I arrive at the airport. As I don't know how my family will receive me.

I left South Africa rich with talent, with a bright

future. I come back with nothing, my life in pieces and covered in guilt and shame".

Few weeks later, it was now certain that Jeremiah would return home. It was a Friday late afternoon. His parents were made aware that he was returning for good. As we were standing at Cape Town International airport, waiting for his plane to land, I could sense the anxiousness from both his parents.

It was time, the aircraft had landed, it was now time for Jeremiah to walk through the arrivals any moment, and as he walked through with guitar and baggage in his hands, his father sprinted towards him. It was one of the most powerful moments to witness. A father and son embrace without uttering a word. It was the full process of restoration in one powerful moment.

Yes, Jeremiah messed up, but the love of his father was greater than the mess.

Chapter Fourteen

THE OLDER BROTHER, PART 5

The story of the prodigal son doesn't make everyone happy. The older son didn't leave home, but if you read the story carefully, you'll discover that he too left his father. As the scene opens, where is the older son? He's out working in the field.

There are two mentions of the older son in the opening of the story. As Jesus begins the story He says,

> "There was a man who had two sons. The younger said to his father, 'Father, give me my share of the estate.' So, he divided his property between them". – Luke 15:11

In the first sentence, he's mentioned as an object, as one of the two sons. In the second, he's mentioned as having received his share of the estate. "He divided his property between them."

The older son owns everything that he and his father now live on. It belongs to him.

As the older son returns from the fields, he is met with a party atmosphere, He is confronted with music and gets the report from one of the servants that his younger brother has returned home safely and that a party is happening.

What's the older brother's response to this? He becomes enraged and is filled with anger.

He refuses to join the party. This act would be a severe insult to his father, and humiliate him a second time in front of the whole community. In Jewish culture, the older son's role at a party was to welcome all the guests. With him not at the party, everybody would know that he rejected his father.

If you read further, you find that, in his heart, the older son has distanced himself as much from his father as the younger son.

It is possible that you can be in church, attend all the activities, yet be disconnected from God.

> *He says to his father, "Look! All these years I've been slaving for you and never disobeyed your orders. Yet you never gave me even a young goat so I could celebrate with my friends". – Luke 15:29*

Those two statements give us clarity to the older son's distance from his father.

First, does he think of himself as a son? No, he's been slaving for the father. He hasn't lived with him like a son, but like a servant. This was the very thing the younger son had decided in his heart he would become after he caused his father shame.

Second thing, he's mad because the father had

never given him an animal to throw a party with his friends. Notice that, in his mind, his friends are not the father's friends. He doesn't want to party with his dad or be friends with his friends. He's developed his own relational web, and the father has nothing to do with it.

The saddest thing though about this son, is that he felt deprived by the father because the father had never given him anything – no calf, no chicken, not even a goat.

> *But what happened when the younger son left? The older son got his share of the inheritance too.So, the father says, "My son, you are always with me, and everything I have is yours". – Luke 15:31*

"I already gave it to you! All these years it's been yours".

The older son has distanced himself. And he refuses to join his father at the party. What does the father do? The same thing he did for his younger son – he humiliates himself by leaving the party and going out to his older son.

Jesus in the parables uses a chiastic structure; this is a literary technique of repetitive symmetry, designed to create insight and resonance through both comparison and contrast.

As this story is told by Jesus, I want to suggest to you that Jesus is doing something very deliberate with this story, that would have been intuitively understood by all his listeners, because all of them would have used this structure in all of their stories, and the only kind of stories they had ever heard were stories with this kind of chiastic structure.

There's a lack of resolve to the story. In their minds, there's a piece missing. The piece is? What the older son did.

In the first story, a son is disconnected, lost and in wild living, but in the end, he is found. In the second story, the son is disconnected, also lost, but spiritually.

In the end what does he do? That's the question Jesus poses to the Pharisees at the end of telling them about the lost sheep, the lost coin, and the lost son. Clearly in their minds, they were the older sons. They were the ones who had stayed around and tried to obey and served God like slaves. But in their hearts, they were disconnected. They didn't want to come to the party and celebrate the return of wayward sons who squandered their living in foreign lands. They didn't want to be near the father.

Jesus is saying, "The younger son understands and accepts that he was disconnected and has been found. He admits he was lost. The father comes out to him and outrageously welcomes him back into the home. The older son, he's disconnected too. And he's proud because he knows he's not really all that bad of a guy. He's mad at the father, so he refuses to come in. The father comes out to him, in just as much humiliation as he comes out to his younger son. And he talks about rejoicing, and he asks the son to come in. Does the son come in? Do you come in?"

I have a great love for writing; this includes books, articles and most challenging, theatre productions. So, after Jeremiah returned home, reconciled with his family, we began to speak about working on a new production, The Broken Pieces.

I started sharing it with some friends in ministry and was completely gobsmacked at their responses.

Jeremiah had built some sort of poor reputation as being a reckless individual, but no one knew the redemptive transformation that he had gone through, repenting, and recommitting his life to Christ.

People just shot him down, simply because they based their viewpoint on his mistakes. Like Jeremiah's dad, the father loves all his children so much that he is willing to suffer and be humiliated to bring us home.

Chapter Fifteen

THE ONE

15 "Now the tax collectors and sinners were all gathering around to hear Jesus. 2 But the Pharisees and the teachers of the law muttered, "This man welcomes sinners and eats with them". - Luke 15:1-2

Jesus started off the illustrations addressing the characters he was confronted with right at the beginning.

Tax collectors:
They were the worst kind of guys; Jewish in ethnicity but not in practice; they worked for the Roman government. They were widely known as extortioners. They would overcharge their fellow Jews and pocket the difference. Sounds familiar to the days we are living in.

Sinners
This term would describe people who were not religious and public about their sin. This could include prostitutes & thieves—but also people who just went about their lives without paying much attention to God or the things of God.

Tax collectors and sinners were excluded from the religious community. When a religious person would see them, they would frown upon them.

The Pharisees:
The root of the word means to separate or detach.

They were well known for being a group that came across as holier than thou. They did not spend time with ordinary people. They were also considered the experts in interpretation of the Law; they were well educated around the 1st 5 books of the Bible. So, they weren't anti God or anti Bible—so what was their problem?

Their problem was that they viewed the Scripture through a lens that focused on the sins of others and absolutely blinded them to their own sin. They were your typical religious people, with a "law thinking" response.

The Scribes

They were a sect of the Pharisees. Originally the scribes are seen in the Old Testament as those who prepared and issued decrees of the king of Israel. But by the time Jesus walked the earth, their duties had devolved into 2 activities: making new copies of the Law and teaching their own spin on the law, which in effect subjected the Scripture to their own perspective. They were a mean group.

One night while Jeremiah and I were working in studio, he asked me the question, "how long will I have to prove to people that I have moved on from my mistakes". I couldn't answer as this was true. As the global Church we have done that knowingly or unknowingly. We have segregated people by forming cliques.

How many people in the church feel like outsiders based on how we make them feel through our religious thinking?

The Scribes and Pharisees looked down on those who did not know the law or follow the law with great contempt. And because of that, the Pharisees & Scribes would refuse to eat with them. To understand that completely, you've got to understand what eating meant to those in the ancient near east. There was no fast food, not because fast food hadn't been invented yet, but because a meal was a time of protracted discussion, storytelling, fellowship, of intimacy and transparency. They would linger over a meal for 2-3 hours. If you ate with someone, you communicated to each other that you valued them, esteemed them, and cared about them. No way the Pharisees would be caught dead eating with someone who everyone knew was a low life!

No way Christians would be found dead sitting with sinners - that's maybe not an accurate statement, but are our actions louder than our words?

It's one thing to say that we love all people, but do our actions prove it?

If Jesus, the King over all creation, values the least of these, how much more should we? We should not hold ourselves in higher regard than those whose sins we deem "worse" than ours but love and accept them as fellow members of the church. We are to share in their joys and sorrows and live in harmony with them.

Jeremiah has been struggling to find acceptance in the church, because his earlier life decisions stigmatized how people now viewed him.

How many prodigal sons / daughters are in a distant country (in wild living) because the hearts of the father are turned away from them.

David's wrong decisions caused Absalom to rebel against his father. This was also the same period that David caused his friend Ahithophel great bitterness.

Both Absalom and Ahithophel lost their lives because of David's ill choices.

The prodigal son's father, a direct representation of Jesus, rose above his own personal issues and humiliation, and restored his son.

Simply put - the father's heart was turned to the son, and the son returned to the father.

CONCLUSION

The world needs us to show the love of Christ more than ever. This will stop the surge of attacks of the enemy on the greatest institute that Christ created.

Our families need our fathers' hearts in the right positions. It's time to go after the one.

The prodigal son's father gives us a clear picture of the true Gospel. God is not some disciplinarian that wants to constantly punish us, instead He's a loving father who will do anything to bring us back to Him. Nothing that we do can make us earn the love of the father. We can't earn our way back into a relationship with Father God.

He has paid it all and at a great personal cost! That's the finished work of the cross.

He is constantly looking, taking on the role of a servant, waiting to run to us and freely offering His grace to us. When we accept His grace He then sits down at the table and eats with us to seal that reconciliation.

The question remains at the end of the story – are we willing to accept that God wants to find us? Will we accept being found?

Will we respond to that costly love? Better yet, as ambassadors of this Christian movement we are mandated to adopt the nature of Jesus Christ. For

Christ is love.

> *13 If I speak in the tongues[a] of men or of angles, but do not have love, I am only a resounding gong or a clanging cymbal. 2 If I have the gift of prophecy and can fathom all mysteries and all knowledge, and if I have a faith that can move mountains, but do not have love, I am nothing. 3 If I give all I possess to the poor and give over my body to hardship that I may boast,[b] but do not have love, I gain nothing. – 1 Corinthians 13:1-3*

Our heart position is found in the character and the nature of Christ and His great love for us.

The prodigal son represents:
- The Drug addict
- The Prostitute
- The Thief
- The Sinner
- You and I

Just recently I visited Jeremiah's house and I shared with his father that I was writing this book. I asked him one question to affirm this concept of "Daddy, can I come back home". - Why did you run to Jeremiah that day at the airport? His answer: "Because no matter what he has done, he is still my son, and nothing changes that.

That's true love. It's time for us to get back to that true love.

> *4 Love is patient, love is kind. It does not envy, it does not boast, it is not proud. 5 It does not dishonor others, it is not self-seeking, it is not easily angered, it keeps no record of wrongs. 6 Love does not delight in evil but rejoices with the truth. 7 It always protects, always trusts, always hopes, always perseveres 8 Love never fails. But where there are prophecies, they will cease; where there are tongues, they will be stilled; where there is knowledge, it will pass away. 9 For we know in part and we prophesy in part, 10 but when completeness comes, what is in part disappears. 11 When I was a child, I talked like a child, I thought like a child, I reasoned like a child. When I became a man, I put the ways of childhood behind me. 12 For now we see only a reflection as in a mirror; then we shall see face to face. Now I know in part; then I shall know fully, even as I am fully known. 13 And now these three remain: faith, hope and love. But the greatest of these is love. - 1 Corinthians 13:4-13*

True love is patient
Patient means to be longsuffering, slow to anger, slow to punish.

1. We need to be Patient with those who need to

grow.
2. How can we be Patient with the imperfections of others.
3. Be Patient when mistakes are made.

True love is kind
Kindness means carrying out acts that demonstrate loving kindness.

> *18 My little children, let us not love in word or in tongue, but in deed and in truth.- 1 Jo 3:18 (NKJV)*

> *She extends her hand to the poor, yes, she reaches out her hands to the needy. – Proverbs 31:20 (nkjv)*

1. Love seeks ways to demonstrate itself.
2. Love goes beyond what is "expected".

True love defends
Protection is to preserve, to cover over with silence. Love does not attack, but defends. We are required through love to defend those prodigals.

> *Hatred stirs up strife, But love covers all sins. – Proverbs 10:12*

> *8 And above all things have fervent love for one another, for "love will cover a multitude of sins – 1 Peter 4:8)*

True love believes and commits

16 By this we know love, that he laid down his life for us, and we ought to lay down our lives for the brothers. – 1 John 3:16

Love produces strong commitment. Like that of the Apostles of old who were committed to Christ even to the point of being martyred.

True love trusts.

Trust means assuming the best about someone, not the worst.

9 But, beloved, we are confident of better things concerning you, yes, things that accompany salvation, though we speak in this manner. 10 For God is not unjust to forget your work and [d]labor of love which you have shown toward His name, in that you have ministered to the saints, and do minister. 11 And we desire that each one of you show the same diligence to the full assurance of hope until the end, 12 that you do not become [e] sluggish, but imitate those who through faith and patience inherit the promises. – Hebrew 6:9-12

True love perseveres

> *"Though He slay me, yet will I trust Him. Even so, I will defend my own ways before Him."*
> *– Job 13:15*

> *Therefore I endure all things for the sake of the elect, that they also may obtain the salvation which is in Christ Jesus with eternal glory. – 2 Timothy 2:10*

Perseverance means staying loyal in bad times as well as the good. Just because your prodigal has walked away it doesn't give you the right to change the position of your heart.

True love endures

> *"So Jacob served seven years for Rachel, and they seemed only a few days to him because of the love he had for her." Genesis 29:20*

Endurance means a refusal to give up or give in.

Daddy, can I come back home is not a cry from the prodigals to come back home, instead it's an enquiry as to whether we the Fathers, Mothers, and leaders are ready to run and reconcile a generation that has been disconnected from God and His presence. It's time to run to our generation and win them back with love.

To the prodigals, the ones that were hurt by the institute called the church, the ones disappointed by their parents, the ones that were abandoned by their biological fathers - This is a time to come to your senses as God has repositioned the hearts of our sons to return home.

> *"And he will turn The hearts of the fathers to the children, And the hearts of the children to their fathers, Lest I come and strike the earth with a curse". – Malachi 4:6*

Jeremiah made mistakes, but it was the receptive heart of the father that brought him back into communion with God and the family of God.

To all the Jeremiahs - it's time to go back home.

NOTES

1. https://www.sermoncentral.com/sermons/print?sermonId=109858
2. https://www.sermoncentral.com/sermons/print?sermonId=194721
3. https://www.britannica.com/topic/patria-potestas
4. https://alivecounselling.com/counselling-resources/how-our-family-relationships-impacts-us-the-father-wound/
5. https://www.google.com/search?q=teshuvah+hebrew+meaning&oq=teshuvah&aqs=chrome.1.69i57j0i512l-4j0i20i263i512j0i512l4.1926j0j15&sourceid=chrome&ie=UTF-8
6. https://www.sermoncentral.com/sermons/the-ministry-of-reconciliation-christopher-holdsworth-sermon-on-reconciliation-181567
7. https://www.americamagazine.org/content/the-word/welcome-sinners

www.ingramcontent.com/pod-product-compliance
Lightning Source LLC
Chambersburg PA
CBHW071859020426
42331CB00010B/2582